HAL LEONARD
BASS METHOD

BLUES BASS

BY ED FRIEDLAND

To access audio visit:
www.halleonard.com/mylibrary

Enter Code
6332-8353-7326-1168

Guitar pictured on cover courtesy of Mequon Music

ISBN 978-0-634-08935-0

HAL•LEONARD®
CORPORATION

7777 W. BLUEMOUND RD. P.O. BOX 13819 MILWAUKEE, WI 53213

In Australia contact:
Hal Leonard Australia Pty. Ltd.
4 Lentara Court
Cheltenham, Victoria, 3192 Australia
Email: ausadmin@halleonard.com

Visit Hal Leonard Online at **www.halleonard.com**

INTRODUCTION

Welcome to the Hal Leonard Blues Bass Method. The goal of this book is to teach you the most important aspects of blues bass. Blues bass playing is essentially a simple thing; the key to your success is knowing the various blues forms, rhythms, lines, intros and endings, and most important, having a feel for the music. The technical demands of this style are not great, but the ability to feel the groove is critical; blues is all about the feeling. Blues is the starting point for jazz, R&B, and rock, and its influence can be felt in every style of popular music. It came up from the Mississippi Delta and spread throughout the South, eventually making its way to Chicago where it was electrified in the post-WWII era. Great blues masters like Muddy Waters, B.B. King, Albert King, Freddie King, and Little Walter (among many others) developed their own unique voices within the blues style, each putting his individual stamp on the music. Part of being a good blues bassist is being able to recognize the subtle differences of each artist and region, being able to find the right line, and being willing to stick to it. While the blues is still growing and changing, there is a strong history and tradition in the music that needs to be absorbed and honored. In addition to learning the material in this book, it's very important for you to listen to as many different blues artists as you can. Once you know what to play, it all comes down to how you play it. The depth of your groove comes from your personal internal understanding of the music as a whole—it's not just about the bass—in fact, the bass is there to support the other musicians. A bass solo is a rare occurrence in the blues. Instead, you must learn to derive your fun from the ecstasy of the groove, the perfect meshing of drums, bass, rhythm guitars, and keyboards behind a soloist that is testifyin'!

ABOUT THE AUDIO

Playing with live people is where you learn the most about the blues feel. The audio tracks are included to give you the chance to groove while you're learning the material. The tracks are recorded with a split mix: the left channel has all the instruments, and the right is minus the bass. To hear the bass part, listen to the left channel, but once you've learned it, turn off the left channel and play along with right. This gives you the chance to BE the bass player and lock in with the drums. Special thanks go to Ralph Gilmore for playing those hard-groovin' and consistent drum parts. He's the only drummer I can imagine being locked in a small room with for ten hours and still like! The guitars I all played myself. Many years before I played bass, I was a student of blues guitar. Recording the audio was a welcome chance for me to reconnect with that part of my musical life. Special thanks also go to Line 6 for creating the Variax guitar; every guitar sound you hear on the audio is from that one instrument.

EQUIPMENT

You can play the blues on any bass you have, though some instruments may be better suited to producing the classic blues tone than others. The traditional bass of choice is undoubtedly the Fender Precision, though the Jazz Bass is also widely used. Other basses will certainly work fine; the key is getting a dark, bottomy tone

that will create a big cushion without sacrificing the punchy attack needed to drive the band. Passive electronics are generally preferred for their natural presence, but an active EQ circuit can be used effectively to enhance the low end and cut the treble. While roundwound strings are totally acceptable, flatwound strings like the LaBella 760FM set give you the fat, round tone associated with blues bass. A nice trick to shorten the decay time of the note is to shove a piece of foam under the strings by the bridge. Cut a piece that pushes up against all the strings; this simulates the string mute that was standard equipment on the old Fender basses.

The ideal blues rig would be a tube amplifier like a Fender Bassman 300 with eight 10" speakers, but almost any amp can be dialed in to get the blues sound—remember, we want a full bottom and not much treble. Before you start cranking up the bass tone control, try cutting the treble back and raising the volume. Adding too much bass will strain your speaker's capabilities at performance volume. Experiment and see how much your amp can handle; just don't overdo it. Too much bottom also makes the band's mix too mushy. If you have a modern speaker cabinet with a tweeter, see if you can turn it off; the extreme high frequencies brought out by a tweeter aren't necessary for traditional blues playing.

THE BLUES SCALE

When we talk about scales and chord progressions, we use a numerical system based on the major scale. The familiar do–re–mi–fa–sol–la–ti–do of the major scale gets replaced with scale numbers 1–2–3–4–5–6–7–8.

C MAJOR SCALE

Practice the major scale thoroughly and get familiar with the locations of the numbers in relation to the first note, or "1."

The **blues scale** is the building block of blues music. It is the basis for melodies, guitar licks, bass lines, and even chord progressions. Numerically, it is constructed 1–♭3–4–♯4–5–♭7–8. The ♯4 may also spelled as a ♭5 as a matter of convenience as you can see in measure 3 of this example: the blues scale in E starting from the open E string.

E BLUES SCALE

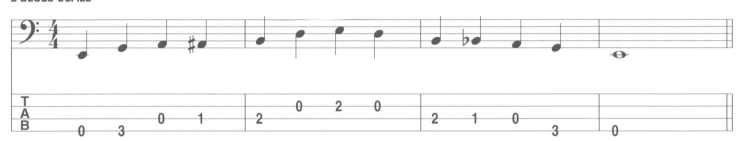

Here is the blues scale in A built from the fifth fret of the E string. This "closed position" fingering (using no open strings) can be moved around the fingerboard to produce a blues scale in any key. You can also play an A blues scale starting with the open A string using the same fingering as the E blues scale.

A BLUES SCALE

THE 12-BAR BLUES FORM

Before we learn specific bass lines, it's important to get an understanding of the blues form. The **12-bar blues** is the most common form in blues, jazz, rock, Latin, country, and other styles. There are other blues forms we'll learn later, but for now let's examine the standard variations of the 12-bar.

The blues progression uses chords built off the 1st, 4th, and 5th scale degrees; that's why they are referred to as the I, IV, and V chords. This first example is known as the "long I" form. The I chord lasts the first four measures in this form. Notice the repeat sign in the last bar. When there is no opening repeat sign before it facing the other way, it's implied that you repeat the entire chart from the top.

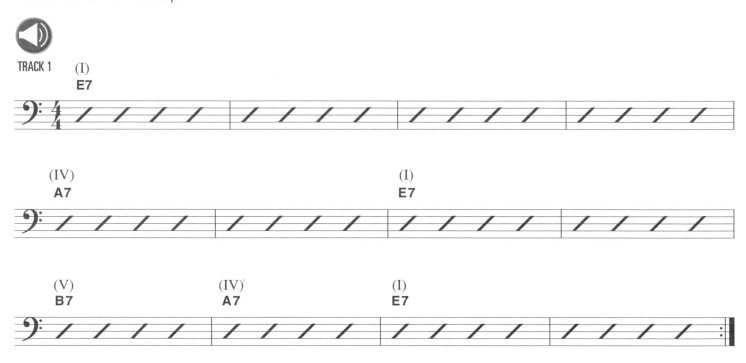

The second 12-bar variation is called a "quick IV." The IV chord pops up in measure 2, and we switch back to the I in measure 3. Sometimes, the melody or vocals of a tune may be a "long I" form, but the "quick IV" form gets used for solos; you need to be able to hear the change and adjust.

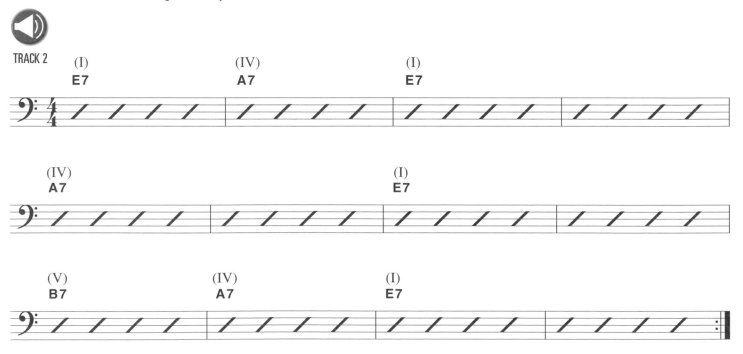

THE SHUFFLE RHYTHM

Most blues uses a rhythmic feel called the **shuffle**. The shuffle hits on the first and third beats of an eighth-note triplet, leaving the second beat alone.

First, practice dividing the beat into triplets. Count this example aloud; make sure you spread the word "tri-pu-let" to fit evenly in the space of one quarter note.

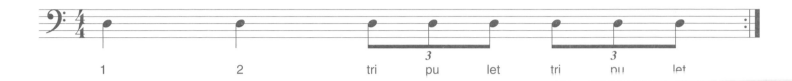

To create the shuffle rhythm, don't play the second beat of the triplet. This example is a "short" shuffle. The second beat is a rest, creating a nice tight feel. Damp the string by slightly lifting your fretting hand to play the rest.

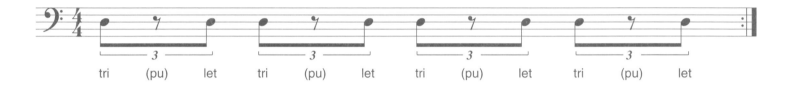

This next example is a "long" shuffle. The first note is held through the second beat of the triplet; the third beat gets played the same. This gives the groove a nice open feel and works well when the drummer plays on the ride cymbal.

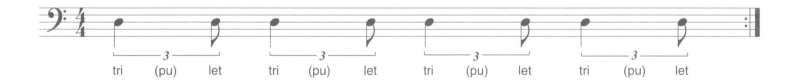

To simplify things, we will notate the shuffle rhythm with this symbol at the top of a song.

Shuffle

Long shuffles will look like regular eighth notes, short shuffles will have staccato marks over the first measure, and the short/long shuffle will have staccato and tenuto marks.

Shuffle

Long Shuffle   Short Shuffle   Short/Long Shuffle

TURNAROUNDS

The last two measures of the blues form contain what is called the **turnaround**, a short progression that ends the form and sends you back to the beginning. As you saw in the first two examples, it is possible to just sit on the I chord for the last two measures. This certainly works fine, but many tunes use specific turnarounds, and guitarists will often use one or the other spontaneously, sometimes even switching around within one tune. Learning the different turnaround possibilities will help you manage the variables of this critical moment in the blues form. The following examples start at the last four measures of the blues form, from the V chord.

This first turnaround is a classic and probably the most widely-used turnaround progression. The bass line walks up through A7 (IV) to B7 (V) and has a syncopated kick that everyone hits. All these examples use the shuffle feel.

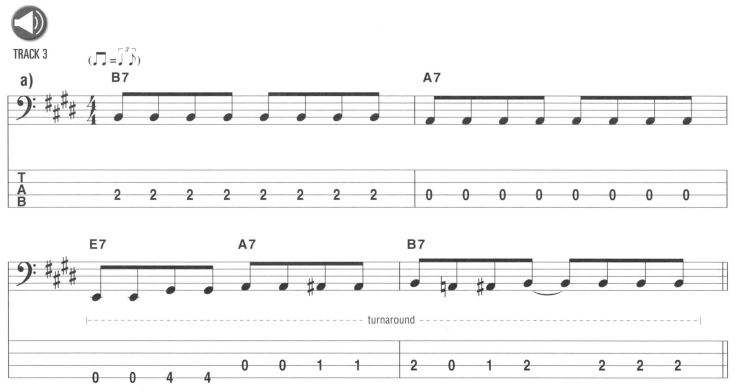

This next one uses the same progression, but walks down from the higher E.

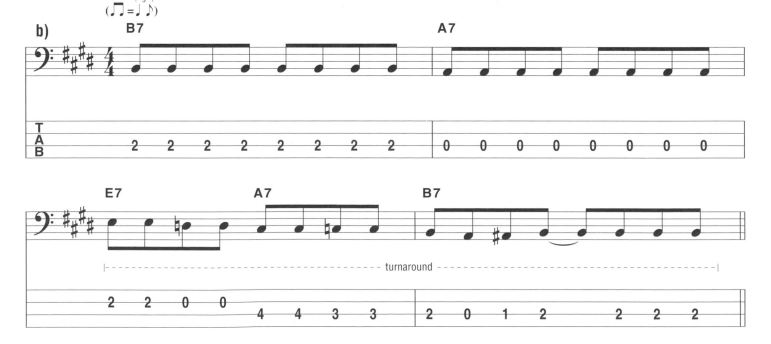

This turnaround is very similar to the last one, except it jumps to the descending line from the low E. There is a triplet fill on the very last beat that can be applied to any of these turnarounds.

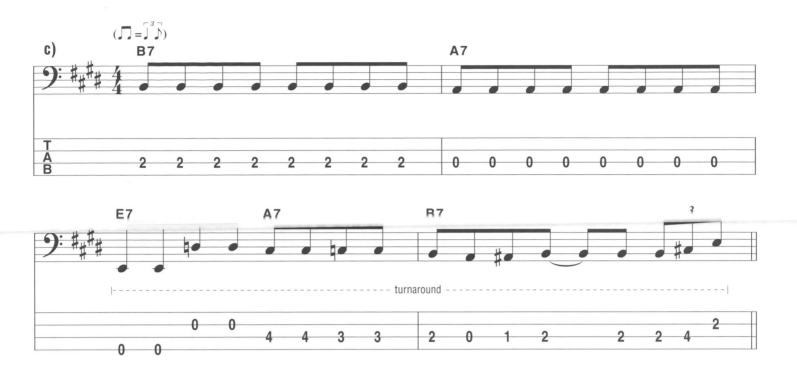

This example goes back to E7 (I) in the last measure and hits the same rhythm kick as the previous turnarounds.

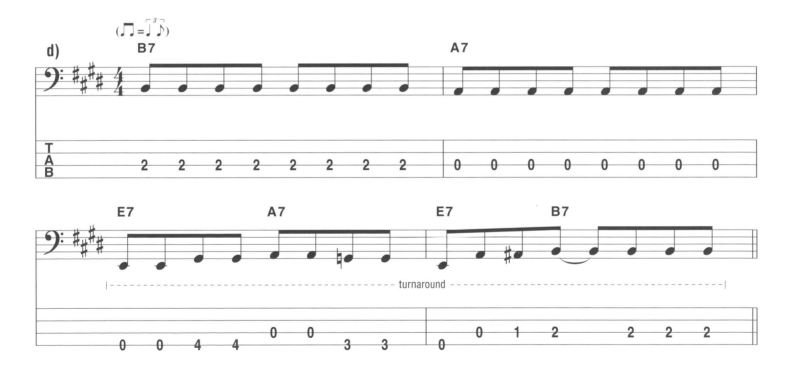

This turnaround stays on the E7(I) chord for the second-to-last measure and catches the rhythm kick in the last measure on the B7 (V) chord.

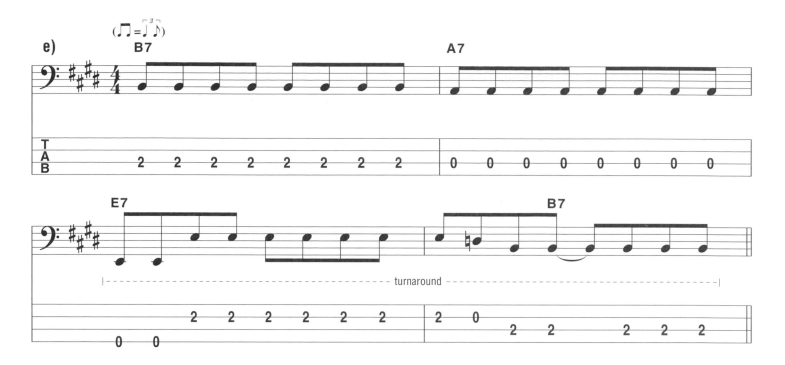

Using the same progression as the last example, we play a descending blues scale in the second-to-last measure for more melodic interest.

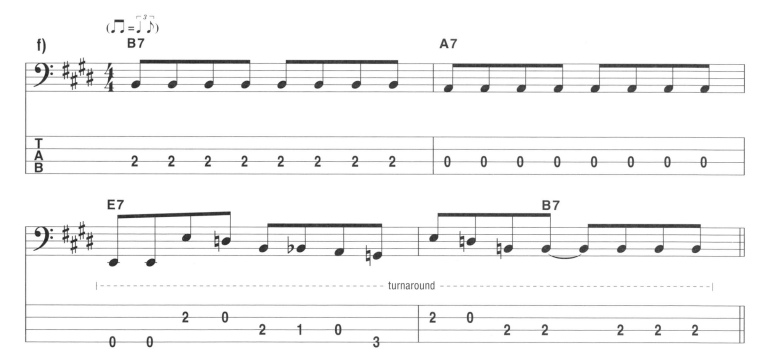

Here is an active turnaround. It's a lot of notes, but sometimes that's okay.

Notice that all the previous turnarounds catch the rhythmic kick on the "and" of beat 2 in the last measure. For most turn-arounds this is the case. Examine these turnarounds carefully. They work in any key. Guitar-based blues bands tend to play in E, A, D, G, and C, and horn-based blues bands will add F, B♭, E♭, and A♭. Be prepared to change the key of any blues tune at a moment's notice.

LAYING DOWN THE ROOT

While there are many cool lines to play, one of the simplest and most effective approaches to the blues is to simply play the root of each chord with either a straight quarter note or shuffle rhythm. At first glance, it may not seem all that interesting, but the deeper you relate to the feel of the music, the more fun playing simple, grooving bass lines will be.

This blues in A stays mostly on the root. After the long I chord, we use a little "walkup" line to move to the IV. After 2 measures of the IV, we use the C♮ to give us a "step down" back to the I chord. Sticking to the root for the V and the IV (with the step-down note back to the I), we have another walkup to the V for the turnaround.

TRACK 4

The use of walkup lines to move from one chord to the next is a classic approach in many styles of bass playing. They create the feeling of forward movement and give the bass line a strong sense of destiny. You can also "walk down" to a chord. Experiment with this concept on your own. You will notice this idea in use throughout the book.

Now let's use the shuffle rhythm to play the roots. The bass line has been altered a little to show you some options, but either version of the root bass line works fine. There are many ways to use this idea. Notice this time in measure 6 we have a walkdown line taking you back to the I chord; in measure 8 we use a low G as a step down to the root of the V chord. In this example we use the low, open E for the root—it's a great choice, as it's the lowest note you have (on a four-string bass) and it sounds big and full. We add the octave E on the last beat of measure 9 to smooth out the transition to the D7 (IV) in measure 10. We step down to the A7 in measure 11 and use the same turnaround as before.

TRACK 5

Using only the root gives the tune a real "down home" kind of feel—it's the simplest thing you can do and still be functioning. It stays out of the way of the melody and any patterns the guitarist may use, it locks in the rhythm with the drums, and with the right attitude, it grooves hard and nasty.

BOX-SHAPE PATTERNS

Many popular bass lines in the blues style are built from what is known as the "box shape." Examining this pattern on the fingerboard, it's obvious where the name comes from—the notes are almost a square on the neck. Box-shape patterns can be easily moved around the neck to play in any key, and the pattern for the I chord is usually transferred to the IV and V chords as well.

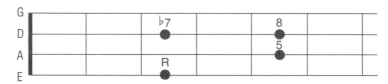

The first box pattern we'll learn is sometimes referred to as the "Uptown Down" bass line. Albert King's instrumental classic "Dyna Flow" is a prime example of this line.

Dyna Flow

TRACK 6

The reverse of this pattern is sometimes called the "Uptown Up" line.

TRACK 7

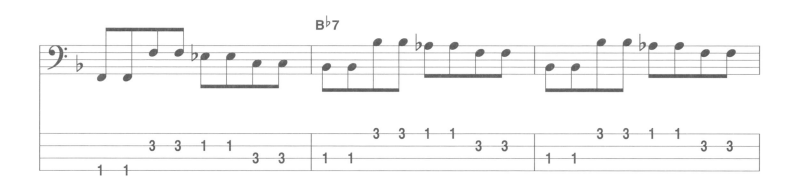

Here are two easy fills that you can add to the Uptown Up and Uptown Down lines. They can be used as a two-measure pattern, or just as a fill before a new chord change occurs.

Another popular blues tune that uses a box-shape line is Junior Wells's classic "Messin' with the Kid." Although the original version does not use a box shape for the bass pattern, it has become common practice in the idiom to use this particular line. There is a signature lick in measures 11 and 12 that serves as an intro figure, a turnaround, and an ending. This tune has a straight-eighths feel and is often played very fast.

Messin' with the Kid
(Higher register)

TRACK 9

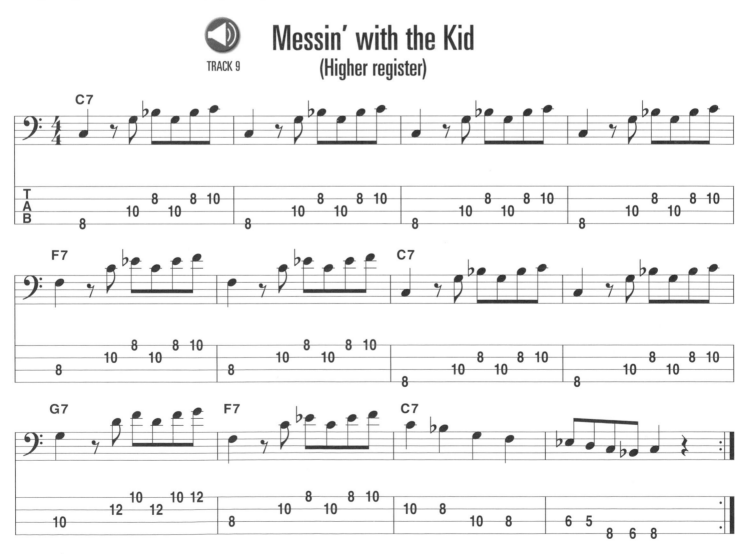

Due to the key of this blues (C), the line has been placed higher up the fingerboard, starting on the eighth fret of the E string. This puts the IV (F7) and V (G7) chords up in the middle register of the bass. This can work just fine, but depending on your taste, or the demands of the particular group, it may be preferable to keep the line in a lower register. In general, it's always a good idea to play in the lower range of the bass, but the key of C is right in the middle, so you can play it moving up to the IV and V chords or down as in the next example.

To play this line with the lower register IV and V chords, we'll need to start on the third-fret C on the A string. This sets us up for easy access to the low F7 and G7 patterns. When you play blues in B, C, Db, D, or Eb, you will have the option to go down to the IV and V, as in this example, or up as in the previous.

Messin' with the Kid
(Lower register)

TRACK 10

Moving up or down to the IV and V is a choice you have as a bass player. You may want to start the tune one way and switch at some point. In general, if you're going to switch the pattern, it's best to wait until a significant spot. For instance, switch after the vocals are done in time for the guitar solo, or switch after the guitar solo for the harmonica solo. Avoid switching in the middle of someone's solo, and certainly don't switch in the middle of the 12-bar form. Part of your job is to be consistent and create subtle changes over time. Repetition plays an important role in blues bass playing.

This box-shape line is typical of the rock/blues style popularized by groups like Cream. This groove is in the style of their hit "Strange Brew."

TRACK 11

Here are a few variations for this line. Just like any box-shape pattern, you can turn it into a blues by fitting the pattern into the blues form. Each variation is played on the track four times.

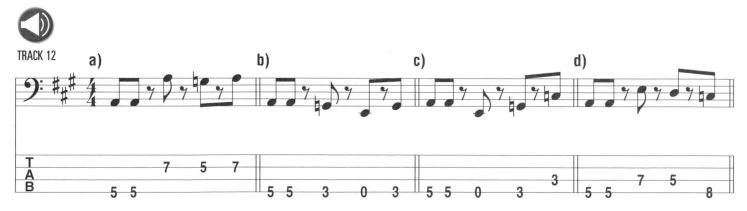

TRACK 12

Here's a version of the previous tune that uses several of the variations. The c) variation forms the main groove on the I chord, and the a) variation acts as a fill in measure 4 to lead to the IV chord. The IV chord uses the b) pattern and then does a walkup back to the I chord. Measure 8 has a walkup to the V chord, which is the Uptown Up pattern, and measure 10 is the a) variation, which leads to a descending pattern to the turnaround. Notice that there is a fair amount of variety in this bass line, yet it functions well as a unit because the variations are all similar and there is enough repetition to establish a uniform sound. While the temptation to "jam out" and play different ideas all the time may be strong, it's best to remain consistent to establish a groove and a framework for the other musicians to play from. This line is a good example of how you can play with variation and still remain functional.

TRACK 13

BOOGIE LINES

Another classic pattern used in blues bass playing is the **boogie line**, derived from the boogie-woogie piano style. There are a few variations, but they all use the 1–3–5 of the I, IV, and V chords. The boogie line is a two-measure pattern that works fine until we hit the V chord. Because there is only one measure of the V, followed by one measure of the IV, we have to split the pattern up to fit the progression.

The first version of the boogie line is configured 1–3–5–6–8–6–5–3. It's played in straight quarter notes, which works with a shuffle, swing, or straight-eighth-feel drum part. The bass line can also be played with a shuffle feel. For the turnaround, we simply play the original pattern.

TRACK 14a

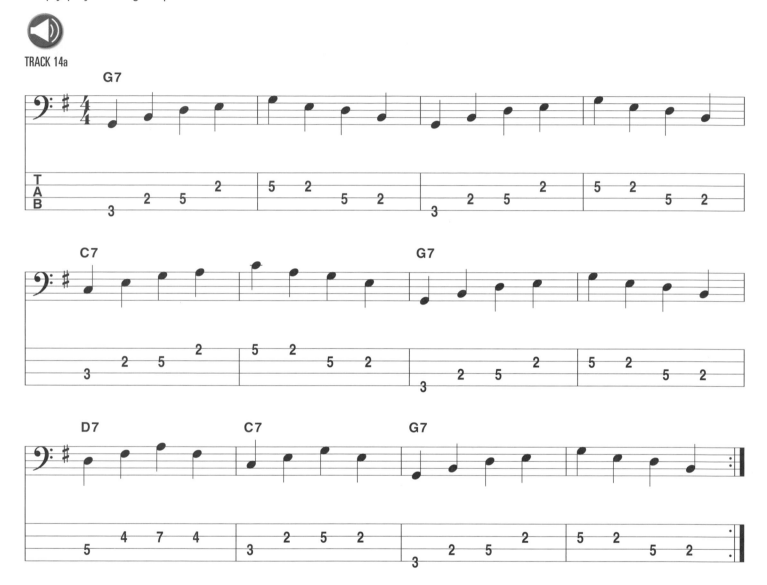

A different turnaround to try walks up to the V chord in measure 12 and back down to the I at the top of the form.

TRACK 14b

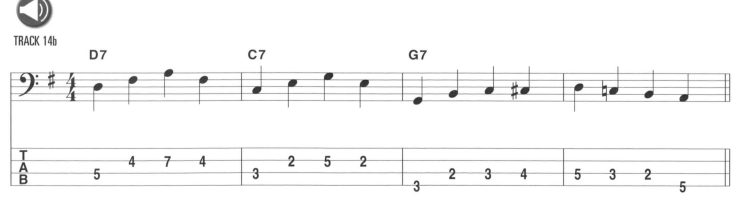

The next version of the boogie line uses 1–3–5–6–♭7–6–5–3 for the pattern. It's one of the most recognized bass patterns in the world. Notice the slight variation in measures 9 and 10. While written out in the open E position, this line will easily transpose to any key.

In the case of a quick IV progression, you have to cut the pattern in the middle of the first measure and switch to the IV chord (playing only the first half of the pattern for the IV). When you return to the I in measure 3, you can continue with the full pattern.

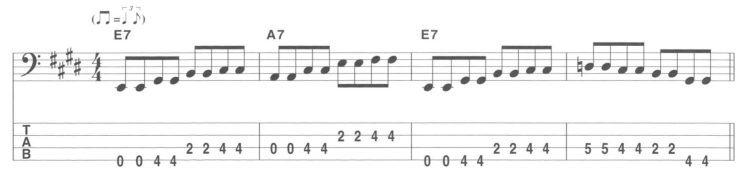

This boogie line is played as a march-shuffle, with staccato (short) articulation. In the key of A, it's possible to play in open position instead of from the fifth fret of the E string. It has a different tone and makes it convenient to use the lower register choices on the IV and V chords (D and E). This line also throws in a triplet fill at the end of each four-measure phrase. It adds interest to the line, and as drummers will frequently play a triplet in this spot, it hooks up nicely with the drum part. Notice how the first two measures only use the first half of the pattern, and then the complete line in measures 3 and 4. This is just another subtle way you can vary the line without getting too far away from the need to be repetitive.

TRACK 16

A Tip on Note Length

It's important to pay attention to the length of your notes. Some of the lines here are written with short articulation, while others are left long. When you are playing with a band, you will need to make this decision on your own. It should be obvious from listening how to approach note length, but a good general tip is to listen to the drums. If the drummer is playing the shuffle on a closed hi-hat, keep your note length short. If the hi-hat is half open, you can lengthen the note a little. If the shuffle rhythm is being played on open hi-hat or the ride cymbal, you can play long notes. It's not unusual for a tune to start with a "tight" feel (closed hi-hat) and then "open up" (ride cymbal) for the solos. In this case, you would need to adjust the note lengths to match up with the drums.

This next boogie line looks very similar to the last one, except it's played with a rhythmic feel that has become associated with blues great Jimmy Reed. His tune "Big Boss Man" is a standard in the blues genre, however it rarely gets played like the original recording. Instead, most blues bass players play a line like this one. It's not straight eighth notes, and it's not a shuffle; it's… a Jimmy Reed feel. Play the first eighth note short and the second one long with a slight accent.

Big Boss Man

TRACK 17a

Here is a sample of the original feel for "Big Boss Man." You may be asked to play it this way sometime. It's more of a country two-beat groove.

The boogie line is extremely well-used in the jump-blues style. Artists like Louis Jordan, Eddie "Cleanhead" Vinson, Big Joe Turner, and others play a style of blues that is closely related to jazz in that it has a swing feel, emphasizes horns instead of guitars, and is typically played in jazz keys like B♭, E♭, and A♭. "Kidney Stew" is a classic jump-blues tune that uses the boogie line with a walking quarter-note feel. Notice the last four measures use a different set of changes: instead of the V chord moving to the IV, we have a iim7 going to the V. This is yet another link to jazz, and the final measures clinch it with the classic jazz turnaround I–VI–ii–V.

Kidney Stew

TRACK 18a

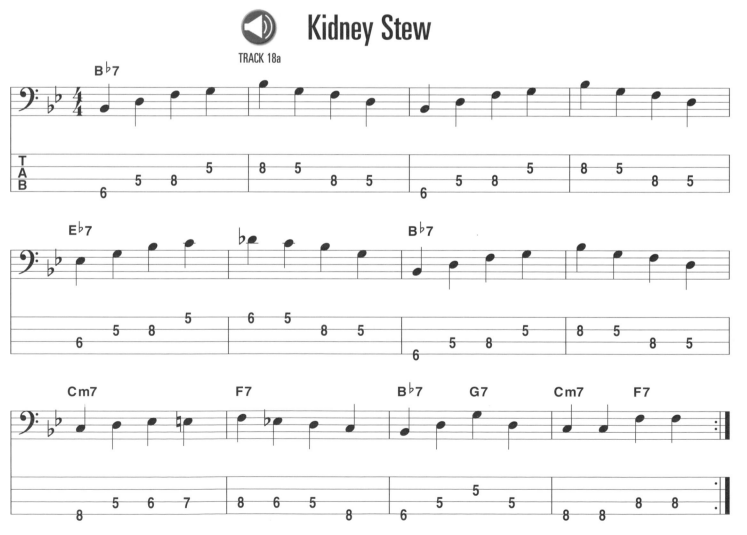

Here's a variation for the last six measures of the tune. It breaks out of position and moves around the neck quite a bit.

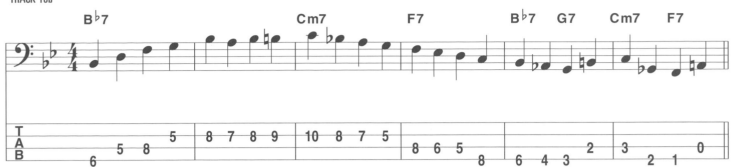

While we're talking about jump-blues, let's look at a cool walking bass line over an F blues. This line works for jump, swing, or jazz. Notice that in measure 7 the line doesn't begin on the root of the F7 chord; it starts on the 5th and walks all the way down the scale to the Gm7 (iim7). This gives the line an extra sense of drama as it works its way down.

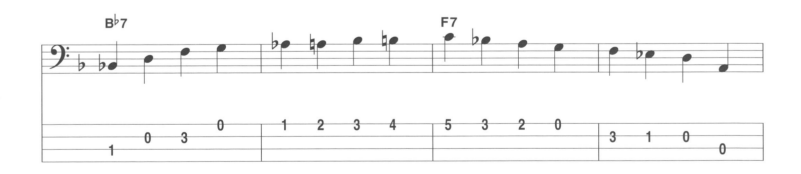

Here's a variation for the last six measures. Notice there are two new chords, Am7 (iii) and D7 (VI), in what would be measure 8. They act as an added "internal turnaround" to set up the Gm7. This is very common in jazz and works great in jump and swing. Notice how the long descending line from the Gm7 to the F7 creates a feeling of destiny.

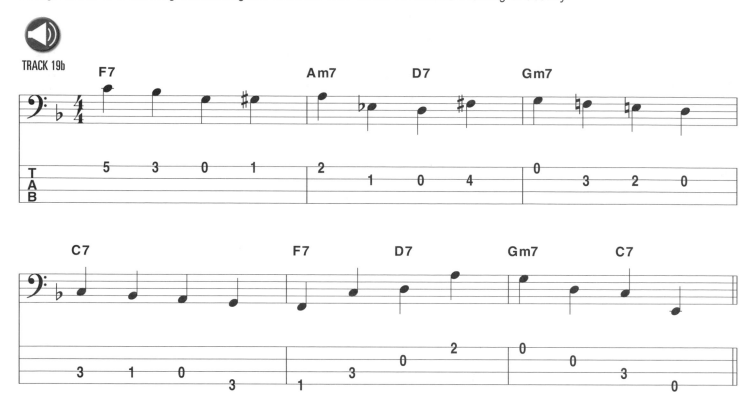

TRACK 19b

SLOW BLUES

At some point during every blues gig, a slow blues is played. It gives balance to a set with all medium and up tempo songs, gives dancers a chance to get close, and most importantly, the singer/guitarist/harmonica player/pianist/whoever gets an opportunity to display some dynamics. Because the tempo is slow, every note you play is very exposed. It's important to play a line that works and that doesn't stick out too much.

This line works well for a medium-slow blues. It uses a 12/8 feel and keeps it moving with a consistent 1–3–5 pattern.

TRACK 20

When playing slow blues, pay careful attention to the soloist. It's typical for the lead player (or singer) to direct the dynamic level of the band to suit their feeling at the moment. They may build up the intensity and suddenly drop way down to create dramatic effect, they may signal for call and response hits, and even stop the tempo completely to hold a note for as long as possible, signaling the return to tempo with a nod of the head or wave of the hand. Make sure your tone stays consistent, and hold your notes for their full length. Leaving holes in your bass line creates a gap that must be deliberate to be effective.

Here's another slow blues with a very different line. It's less of a constant pattern like the previous example; this one rambles around a little more. Notice, however, there is a balance between movement and sitting still. In slow blues, every little move you make is right up front. Don't make the line too active, or you'll take the focus off the front person. In measures 4, 9, 11, and 12, there are eighth-note rests on the second beat. Make sure to leave those spots blank; it creates a gap for the snare drum that is very effective, especially when the drummer sets it up with a crescendo.

TRACK 21

Perhaps the most well-known of all slow blues tunes is T-Bone Walker's famous "Stormy Monday." While T-Bone (and many others) have recorded this tune many times, the version from the Allman Brothers' *Live at the Fillmore* is probably the most widely known. Over the years, this song has become associated with a variation in the chord progression that is a little unusual at first. Even though T-Bone's original version (and many other's as well) follows a straight blues progression, if someone calls "Stormy Monday" on a gig, chances are good they'll want you to play the variation. It's made trickier by the fact that people play these variations differently. This example is a solid version that will work most of the time. If the band you're playing with deviates from this, at least you'll have a starting place to judge how it's different.

Stormy Monday

This chart has a second ending, which replaces the last four measures of the song the second time through. You have to remember how many times you've played the form, think ahead, and be ready to skip over the first ending. The second ending in this case is another commonly-used variation on the last four measures of "Stormy Monday." Besides the A♭7 chord, the bass line gets more active during the turnaround. This activity can be applied to any version of this tune (or any slow blues for that matter).

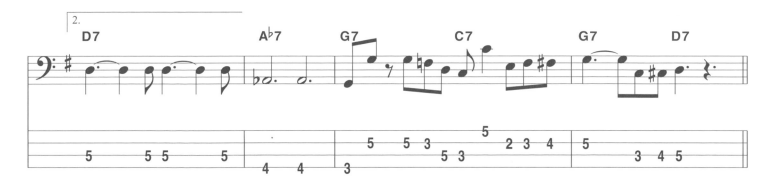

Here is a very cool bass line that sometimes gets inserted in a slow blues. It's a very active line that takes some chops to play well. It's derived from the blues piano classic "Blues After Hours."

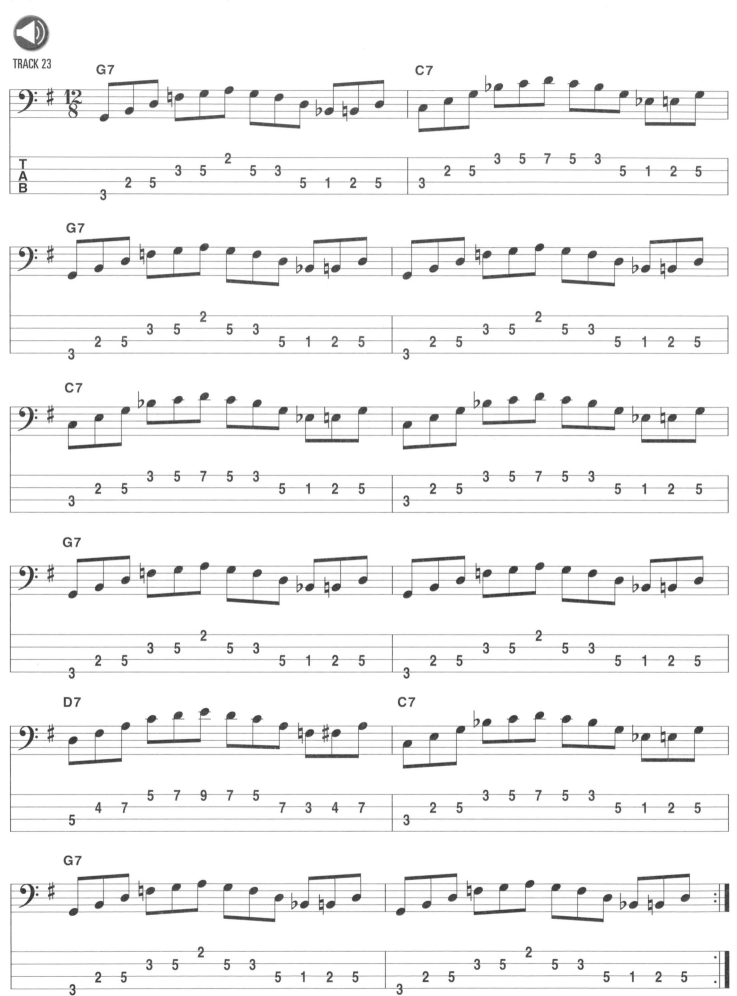

RHUMBA BLUES

The rhumba feel has found a place in the blues style through the New Orleans connection. Many of the early musical influences of blues came from New Orleans, where African, European, Caribbean, and American cultures mixed. Pioneering blues great Professor Longhair mixed Creole rhythms with blues forms and developed a style of blues piano that eventually became the foundation for rock 'n' roll. His heavy left-hand bass patterns set the mold for a rhythmic style that continues to be popular in the blues world. This is the bass line (which is doubled by the pianist's left hand) from his classic hit "Mardis Gras in New Orleans."

Notice that the chord progression stays on the V chord for measures 9 and 10. The stop in measure 10 happens during the vocals and during the instrumental melody. For solos, simply play two measures of the rhumba figure on the V chord.

TRACK 24a

This figure shows up in the more modern recordings of this tune. It's placed in measures 3 and 4 during vocal choruses, or perhaps during a solo to create some excitement.

TRACK 24b

Another classic rhumba blues tune is Albert King's "Crosscut Saw."

TRACK 25

Crosscut Saw

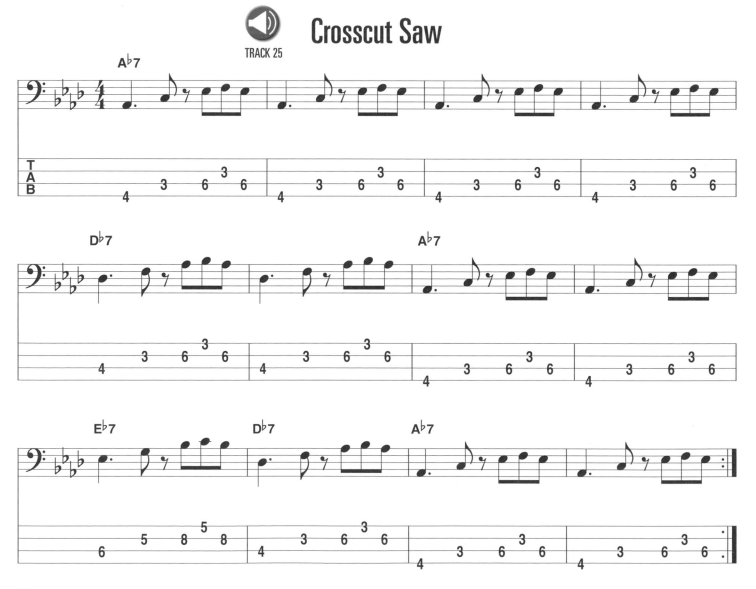

Variations a) and b) have the IV and V chords played down instead of up, and c) is a box pattern that can be used as the main groove.

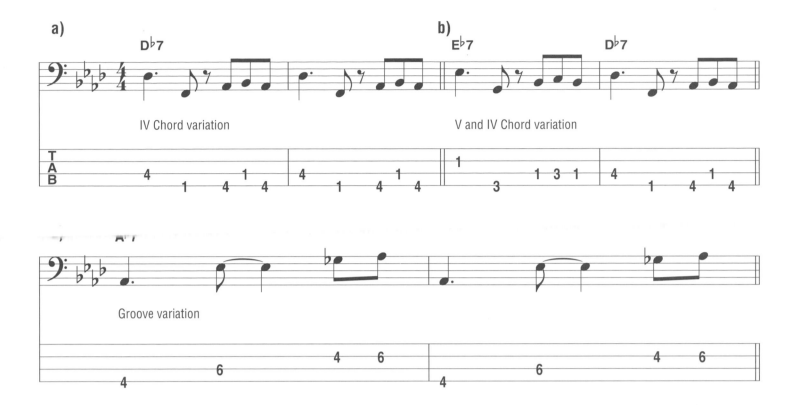

a)

D♭7

IV Chord variation

b)

E♭7   D♭7

V and IV Chord variation

A♭7

Groove variation

INTROS

We've looked at various lines and rhythms to play, but an important part of functioning in the blues style is knowing performance protocol. When a tune is called, some details may be discussed, like the key, the feel, and whether there is a quick IV or long I, but the first order of business is getting into the tune. An intro is a section of music that is placed in front of a song to set it up. Usually an intro is taken from material that is already part of the tune, but in some cases a tune may have an intro composed of new material. There are a few standard blues intros you need to know that are used the majority of the time, especially in jam situations or pickup gigs.

The first and most common intro is called "from the five," or "on the five," simply because you start from the V chord (four measures before the top of the form) and continue on through the tune.

TRACK 26a

This is a classic shuffle-boogie line that starts from the V.

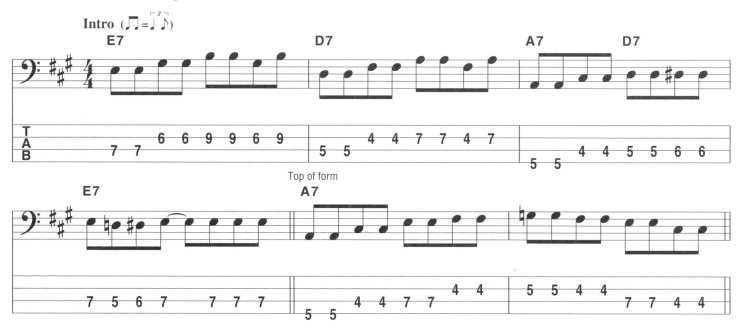

When starting "from the five" on a slow blues, it's common to add these pickup notes to set up the V chord. The countoff will typically be "1...2...3..." with a drum hit on beat 4, and then you play the pickup notes with everyone.

TRACK 26b

This intro is also "from the five," but it places the V and IV chords in the lower register, then goes up to the I chord. This Uptown Up line is actually the intro from Freddie King's classic "Tore Down," which we'll learn in full later in the book.

This one is "from the five" on a Jimmy Reed feel; it uses the same turnaround as the tune.

If the tune is a jump blues with the ii–V change in the last 4 measures, "from the five" will be called "from the two." You are still starting four measures before the top, but the chord is a iim7 going to a V7.

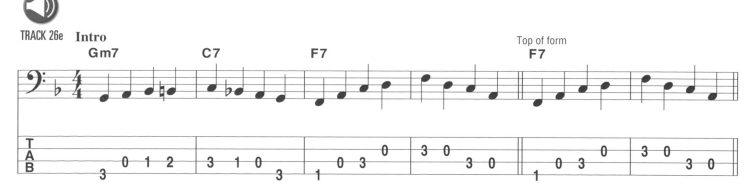

33

Another type of intro that does get called, though less frequently, is "from the four" or "on the four." By now you can guess what that means: start at the IV chord (measure 5), finish the form, and come in with the vocals or melody at the top.

TRACK 27a

Another possible blues intro is "vamp on the one." This means to play the pattern for the tune, whether boogie, box shape, or whatever, on the I chord until the top is cued. This could go on for four measures, eight, or possibly longer. At the end of the vamp a V chord may happen to set up the top, but not always. If you play a V chord when no one else does, it won't do any damage, so it's best to assume you'll play a V. Here's a box shape "vamp on the one" intro, four measures long, with a quick V to set up the top.

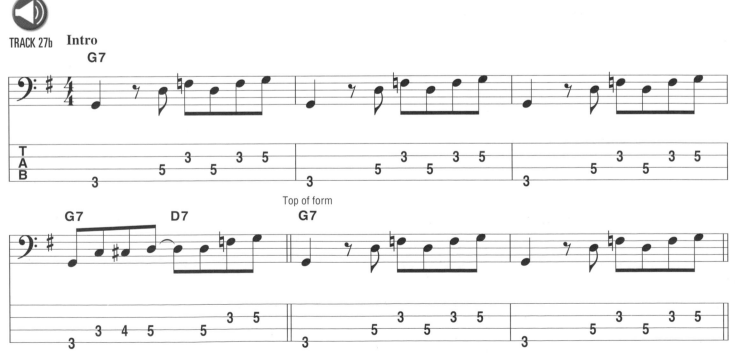

TRACK 27b

T-Bone Walker recorded "Stormy Monday" many times, as has everyone else in the blues. There is a specific two-measure intro for this tune from T-Bone's 1949 recording that often gets played. It starts with triplet hits played by the horns (or guitar) on an E♭7 going down to a D7. The bass comes in on the second triplet of beat 3 in both measures.

TRACK 27c   Intro

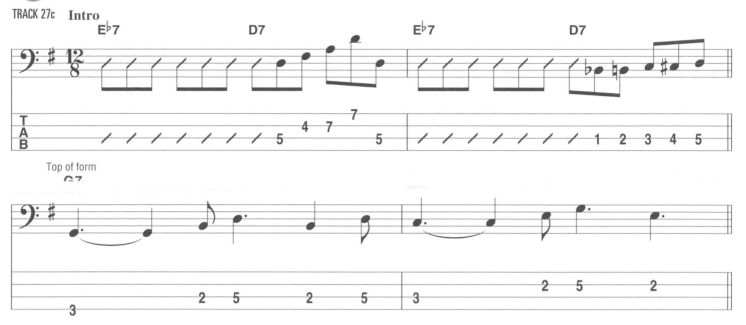

Here's another intro for "Stormy Monday," similar to the one popularized on the Allman Brothers' *Fillmore East* recording. The bass doesn't actually play until the downbeat of the top of the form, but it's important to know how this sounds so you come in at the right spot.

TRACK 27d   Intro

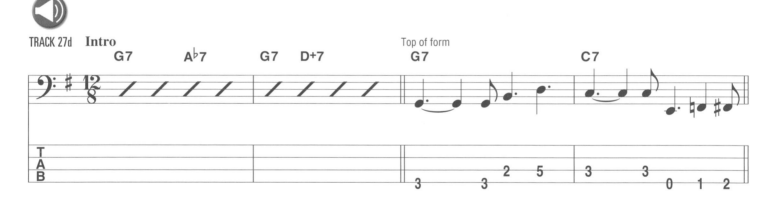

Even simpler, sometimes "Stormy Monday" starts off with just a hanging V+7 chord.

TRACK 27e   Intro

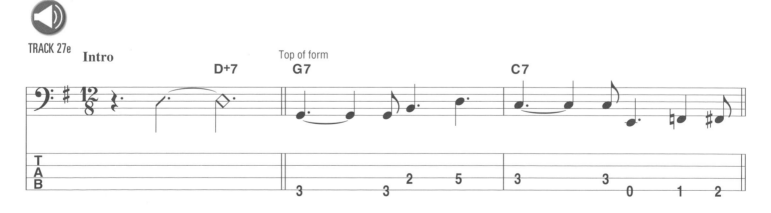

Another very popular intro in blues is to simply play the entire form once through without vocals, perhaps with a guitar or other instrument soloing through it. This is called "once through," and all you need to do is play whatever line the song requires for the entire form.

ENDINGS

No matter how brilliantly a song may be played, if the ending falls apart in chaos, that's what will stick in the mind of the listener—it's the last thing they can remember about a tune. There are several "stock" endings for the blues, and unless you are playing with a set, rehearsed band, you never know which one will get used on any given song. It is rare that the ending will be discussed at the beginning of the tune (you're lucky if the intro gets talked about!), so when the song is over, you'll need to pay attention, looking for cues from the singer or guitarist to see how the ending will take shape.

Here is the most common blues ending: a walkup from the I through the IV to the V, ending the line with the I on the "and" of beat 2. Then hit the I and hold it until you get a cutoff.

TRACK 28a

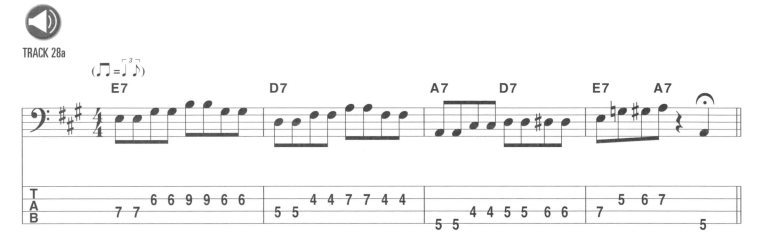

This ending works the same way except it walks down from the I through the IV on its way to the V.

TRACK 28b

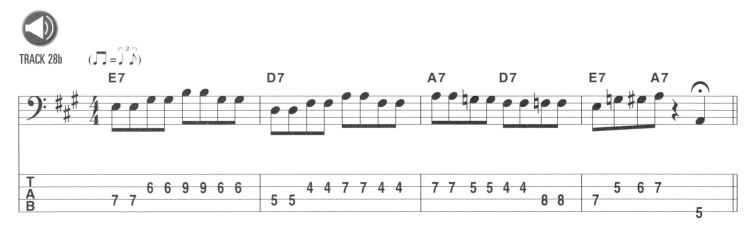

Catch the rhythmic kick on the "and" of beat one, measure 11. This is a common factor in many endings.

TRACK 28c

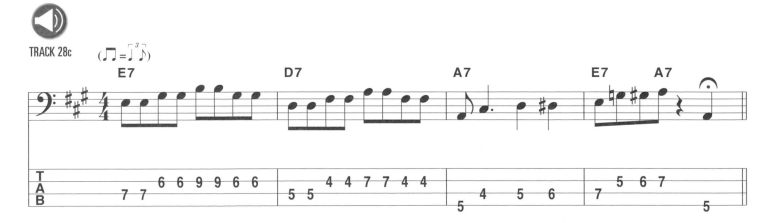

This ending uses the same kick, but works down from the I chord.

TRACK 28d (♫ = ♩ ♪)

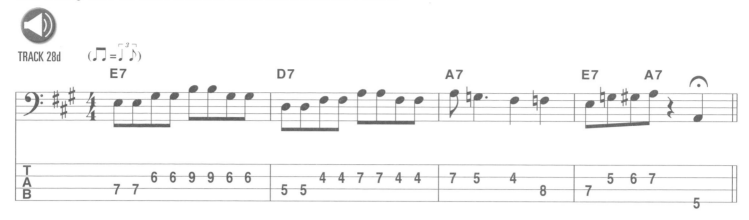

Catching the kick and walking down the scale works great.

TRACK 28e (♫ = ♩ ♪)

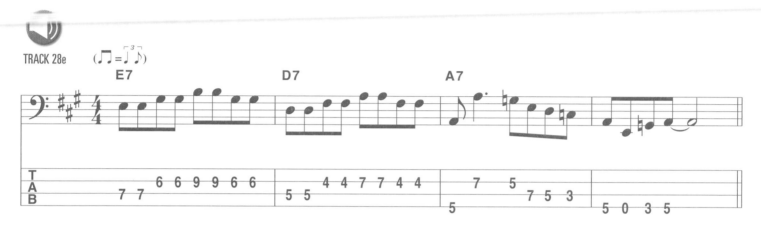

This ending doesn't use the kick, but walks right down the scale. It's common for the band to gradually slow down, or ritard, through the lick.

TRACK 28f (♫ = ♩ ♪)

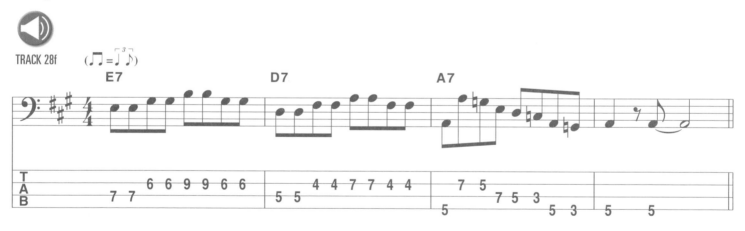

It's very common for the lead vocalist or instrumentalist to cue a stop on beat 1 of measure 10; after that, any of the previously learned endings will work.

TRACK 28g (♫ = ♩ ♪)

STOPS, HITS, AND KICKS

In the blues, there are many different stops, hits, and kicks that are used to create excitement, or perhaps as the main motif for a song. While many of these kicks are tune-specific, there are many standard traditional kicks that get used over and over again.

TRACK 29a

This kick is a classic excitement builder, a chromatic line in quarter-note triplets up to the IV chord. You'll usually get the cue for this in measure 3.

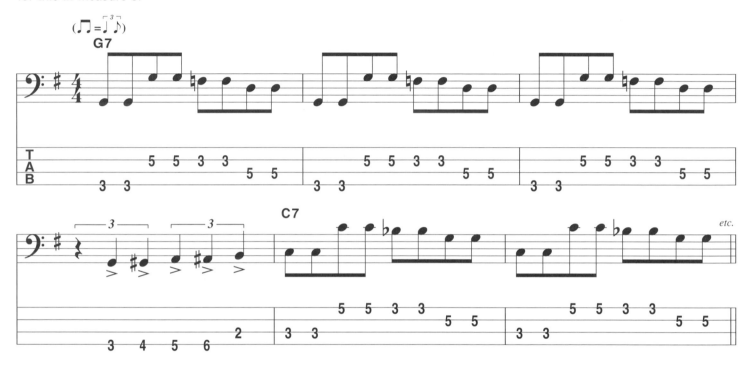

Here's another crowd pleaser, the old "bring-the-band-on-down-behind-me-boys" routine. In a slow blues, use dynamics to create a big buildup to the IV chord. At the IV, the crescendo peaks with a solid hit on beat 2, then suddenly drops to very quiet for the rest of the measure. This will usually be cued by the lead player or singer, and while most common in the shown location, it can happen in other places in the form, usually after a significant chord change.

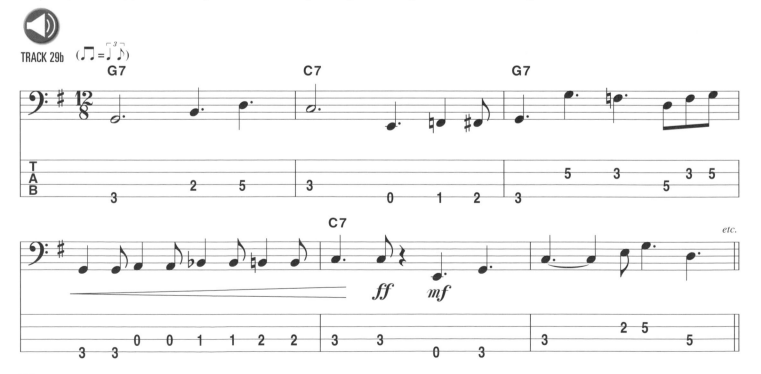

This next routine is a series of stops on the I chord. Many tunes have this built in to the form, but they can also be called spontaneously by the soloist. If it's a singer, they will raise their hand and cue the downbeats; if it's a guitarist, they may just call out to you "stops!" from across the stage or use the neck of the guitar to cue the rhythm section.

TRACK 29c

This set of stops has a triplet pickup. It actually starts at the end of measure 12 of the previous chorus. Notice how the pickup notes come right after the turnaround lick and set up the downbeat at the top. This particular example uses the shuffle rhythm to set up the groove at the IV chord, but you can also play solid quarter notes, triplets, or any number of possible licks.

TRACK 29d

Here is a simplified version of the previous example. It creates a looser feel if the bass player doesn't articulate the triplets.

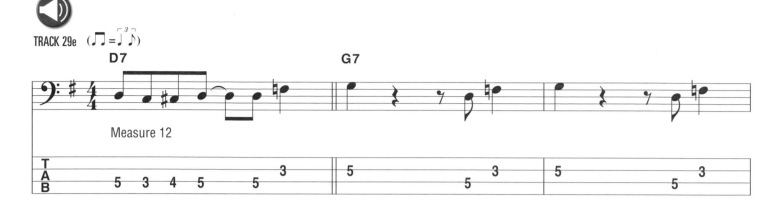

TRACK 29e (♫ = ♩ ♪)

Shown with a quick IV, these stops get the ball rolling again in measure 3 with the quarter notes on beats 1 and 3 leading to a walkup to measure 5.

TRACK 29f (♫ = ♩ ♪)

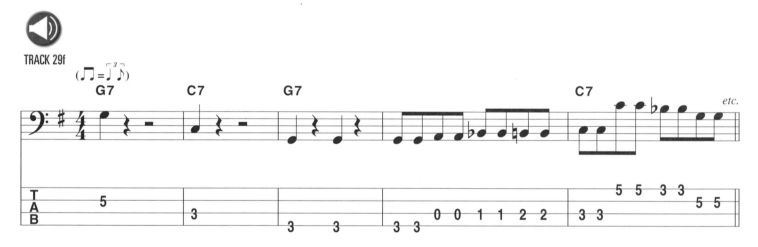

This set of stops uses an anticipation to lead to the next downbeat. It gets back in the groove the same way as the previous example.

TRACK 29g

ALTERNATE FORMS

Although the majority of blues follows the standard 12-bar format, there are variations and alternate forms in common use.

This progression is sixteen measures long and has a gospel flavor to it. Written by the great bassist/composer Willie Dixon, "My Babe" was made popular by harmonica genius Little Walter. On his original Chess recording, there is a faintly audible walking bass line in the background. There is also a low guitar part that often gets used as the bass line, but typically the song is interpreted in a relaxed country-ish two-beat feel. It's marked as a shuffle, but it's more of a swing feel. Give the eighth notes a loose triplet undercurrent.

My Babe

TRACK 30

This is an 8-bar blues. It's the progression for "Key to the Highway," an old Big Bill Broonzy tune recently covered by Eric Clapton. It's also the same progression as "Stack-O-Lee" and "Trouble in Mind."

Key to the Highway

TRACK 31a

Here's a more active version of the last progression.

TRACK 31b

Another blues built from an 8-bar form is "I Hear You Knockin'," however this song also has a second part, or bridge. The 8-bar blues is the A section, and the bridge or B section is a typical eight-measure phrase that starts on the IV chord. The overall form is AABA. This form is often written in charts by using a D.C. (da capo, Italian for "from head," meaning jump back to the top of the page), so that the A section need not be written out again.

In performance, the solo form can go one of two ways. You can solo over a straight 12-bar blues in E and go back to the form for the vocals, or the solos can be over the AABA form. Most often, the vocals will come back in at the bridge. This tune was popularized by Lazy Lester and the Fabulous Thunderbirds. It is not to be confused with the tune of the same name by Dave Bartholomew and other New Orleans artists.

I Hear You Knockin'

A blues with an extended I chord is fairly common: eight measures on the I chord instead of the usual four, then the form plays out like a regular 12-bar blues. This example is a classic New Orleans second line rhumba feel. The last measure goes from the I to the V quickly; it's the most typical New Orleans style turnaround. While this example is very style-specific, the extended I form can be applied to any type of blues feel.

TRACK 33

Performance Tip

To loosen up the feel of this line, try sliding into the A on the F7 chord, the D on the B♭7, and the E on the C7—it adds a little "grease."

BLUES STANDARDS

Here are some standard tunes that get called at jams and gigs all the time.

Every guitar player in the world wants to play Freddie King's instrumental classic "Hideaway." It's basically just a 12-bar in E, but there are some specific feel changes and lines that have to be played in the right spots.

Hideaway

TRACK 34

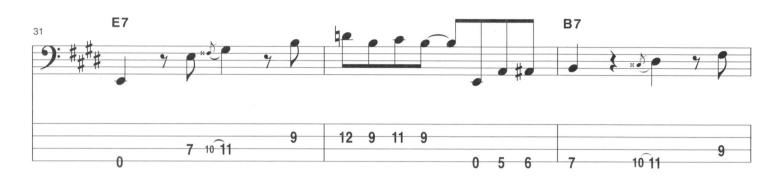

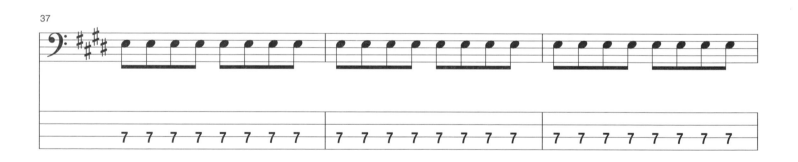

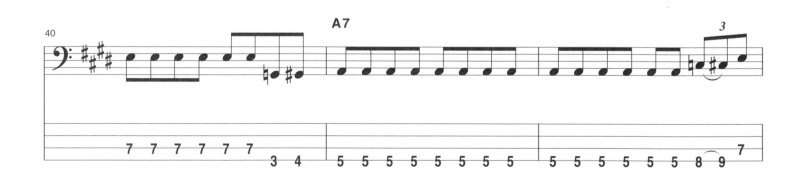

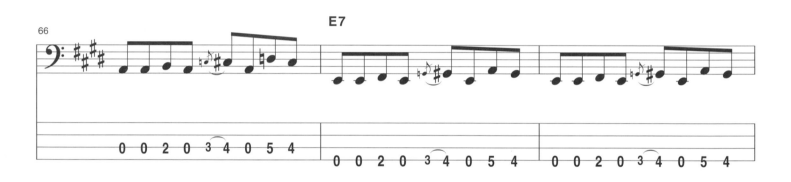

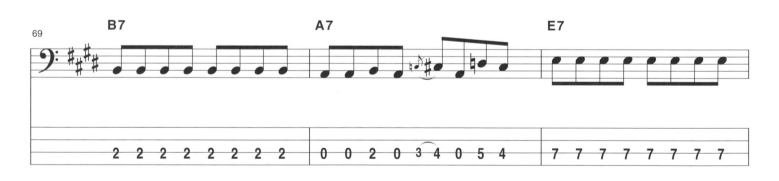

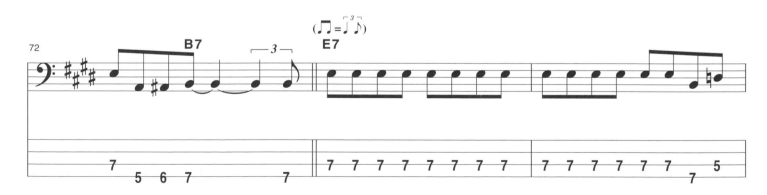

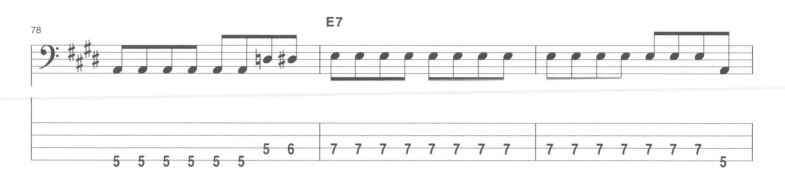

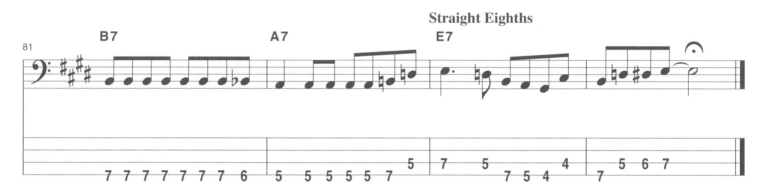

Here's another Freddie King classic, "I'm Tore Down." The tune uses the Uptown Up line, and the intro is "from the five." In the second, third, and fourth vocal choruses there are stops on the downbeats. The third and fourth vocal choruses also have an extended I chord. The ending has a stop in measure 10. This is a very popular tune, so you should memorize this arrangement.

I'm Tore Down

TRACK 35

2nd Voc. Chorus

(bar sax line, optional for bass)

3rd Voc. Chorus

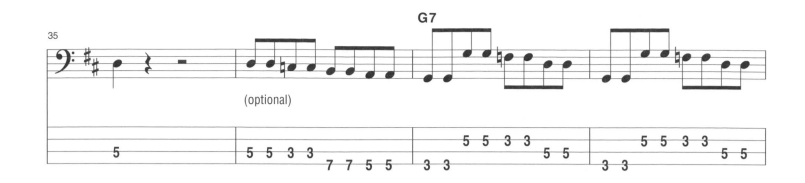

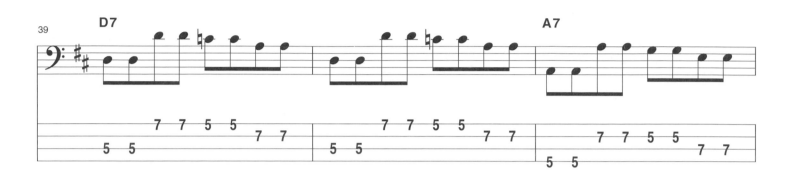

Guitar Solo

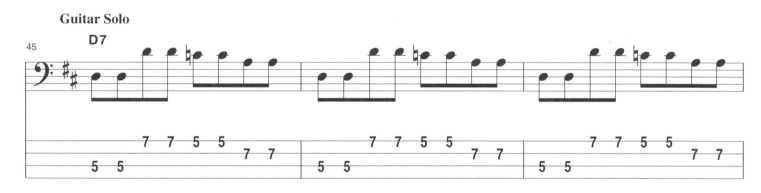

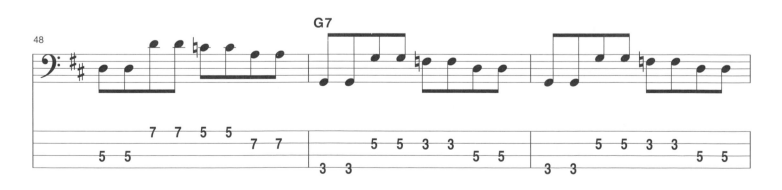

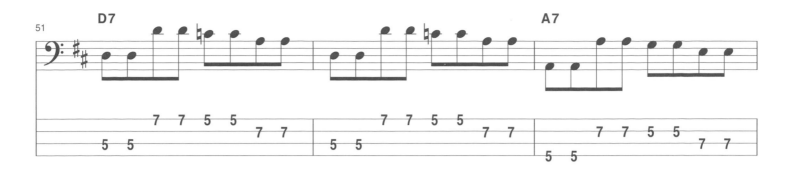

4th Voc. Chorus

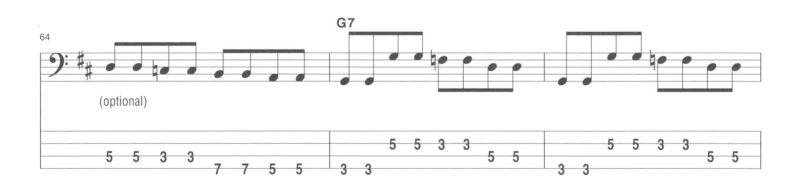

(optional)

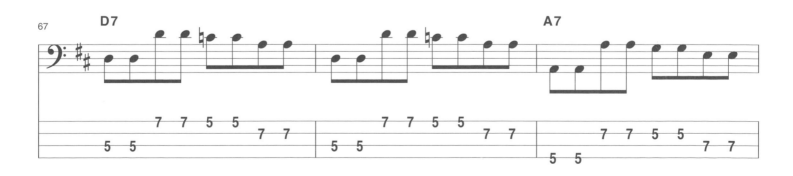

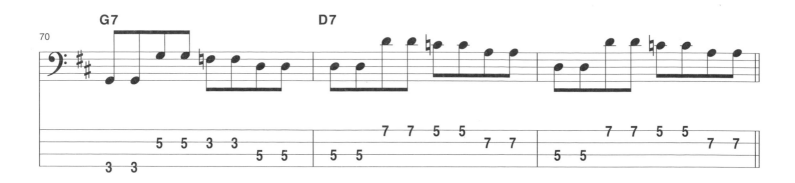

5th Voc. Chorus

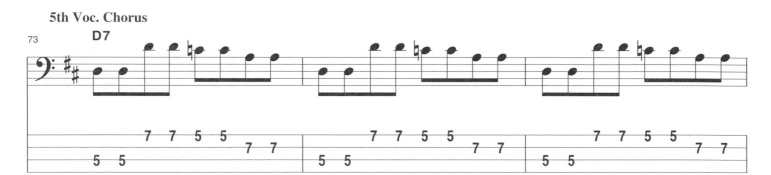

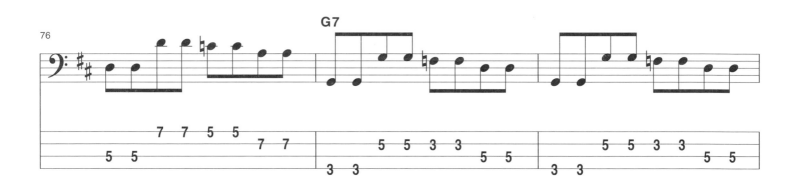

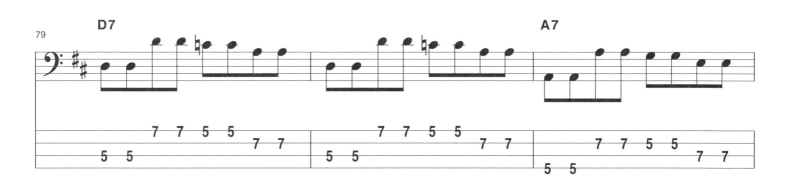

Albert King's "Born Under a Bad Sign" is a standard in the blues genre. It was made a huge hit by Cream and has been covered by many other artists. Albert's original version is a classic. The chorus has an eight-measure form, but the verse is twelve measures. The arrangement has a few tricks, so pay attention to the form.

Born Under a Bad Sign

TRACK 36

Another must-know tune from the blues repertoire is Howlin' Wolf's "Killing Floor." This song was co-opted by Led Zeppelin on their second album and popularized as "The Lemon Song," but the original version is still frequently played. Give the sixteenth notes a lazy feel to really capture the groove on this one.

Killing Floor

TRACK 37

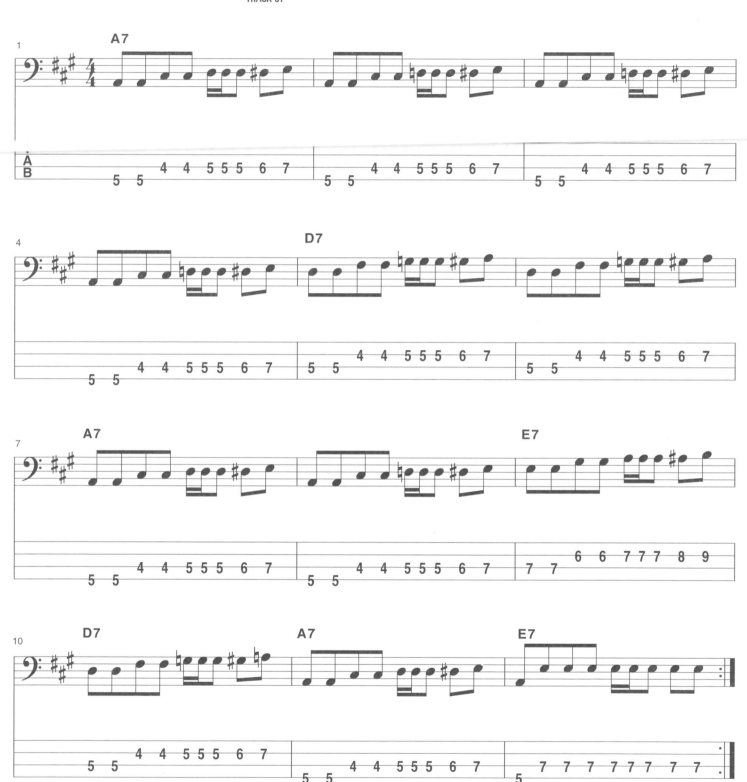

Here's a blues tour de force by the legendary Stevie Ray Vaughan. Bassist Tommy Lee Shannon pulls out all the stops on this one. The main figure is a cool descending line with a bounce to the lower octave open string. There are boogie line figures, box shapes, stops, and machine-gun triplets—a real mix of great ideas. As varied as this line is throughout the entire performance, notice how Tommy holds it together by staying consistent within each 12-bar chorus. When he introduces a new idea, he develops it through the form, then changes it in the next chorus. There is a logic behind the construction of this line that makes it a classic performance.

Pride and Joy

TRACK 38

Tune down 1/2 step:
(low to high) E♭–A♭–D♭–G♭

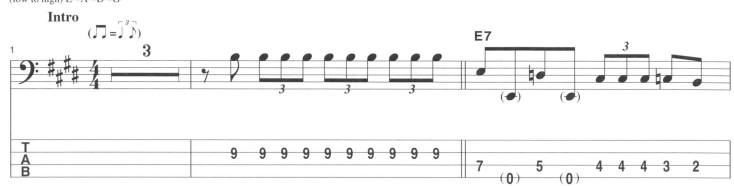

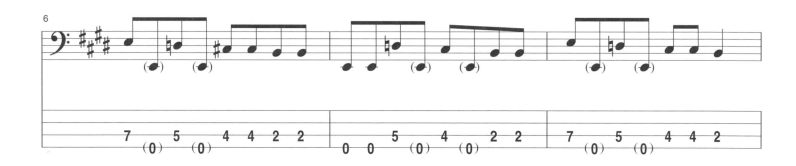

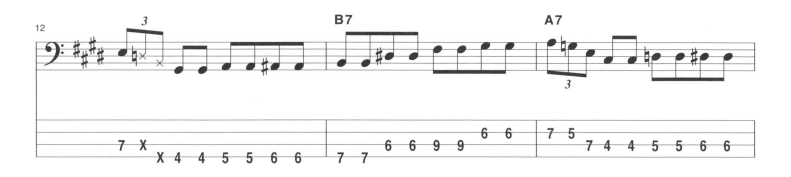

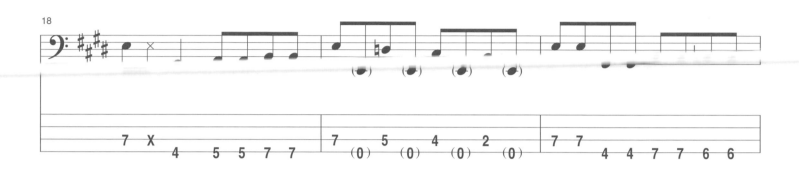

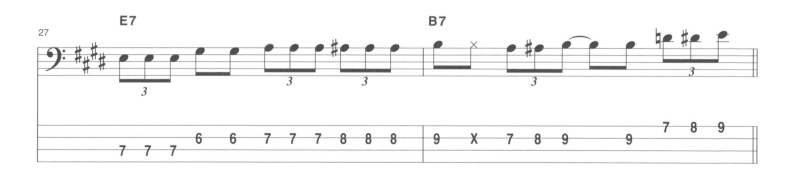

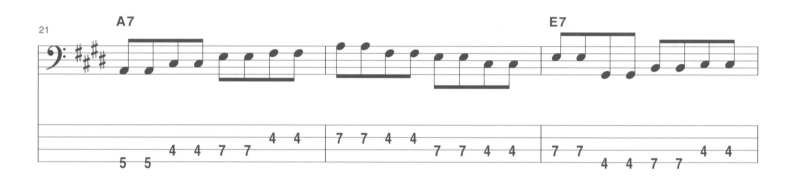

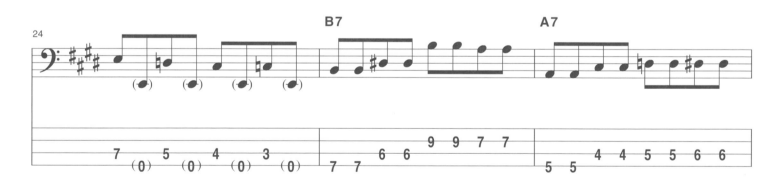

Verse

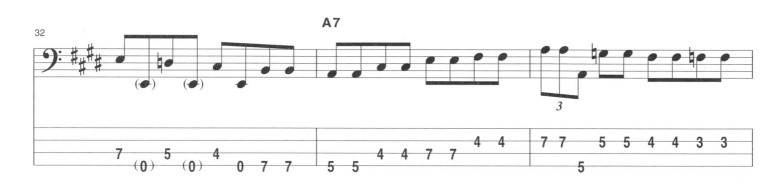

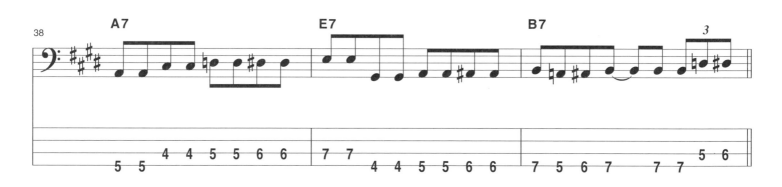

Verse (stops)

64

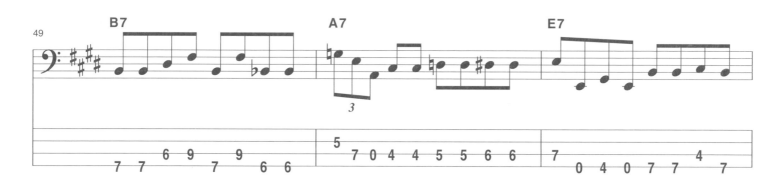

Guitar Solo

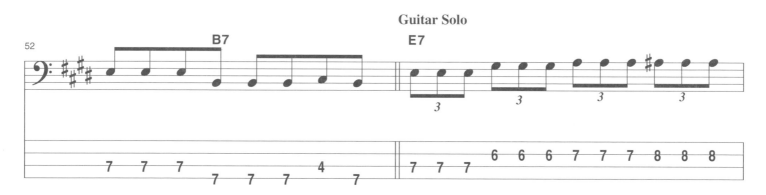

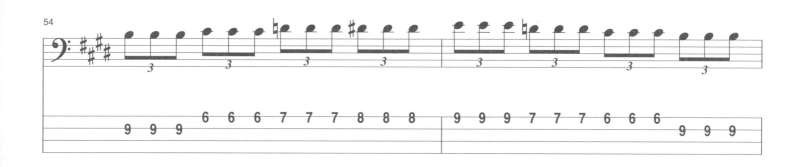

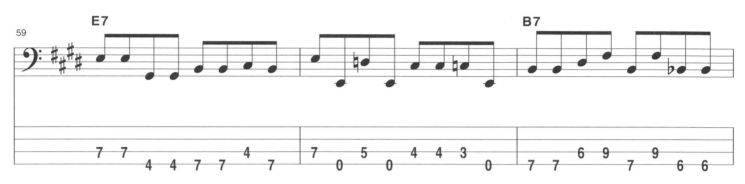

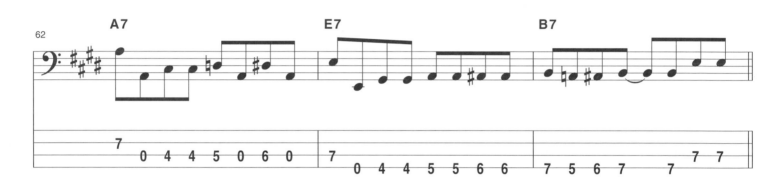

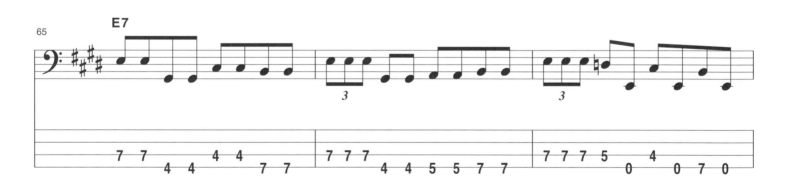

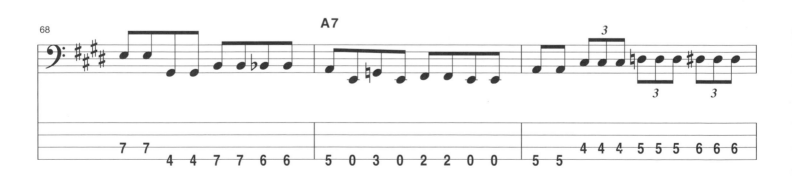

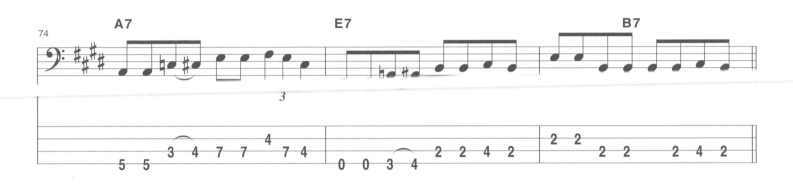

Verse (stops)

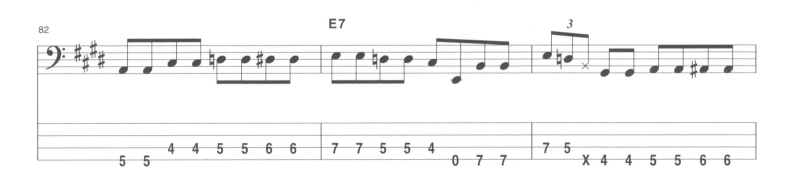

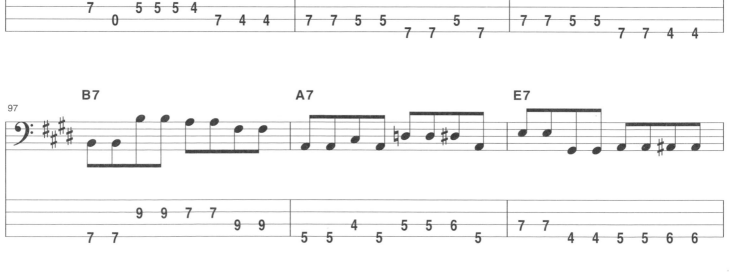

Guitar Solo

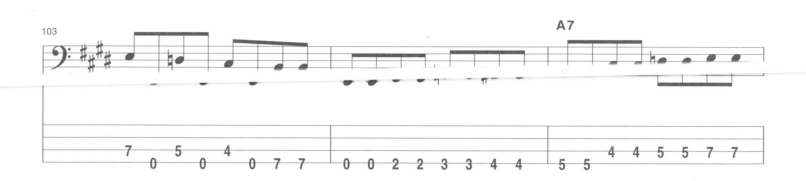

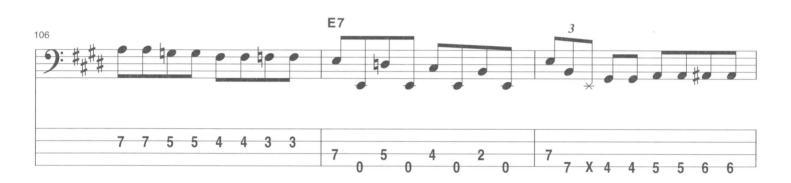

Willie Dixon's "Hoochie Coochie Man" was made popular by Muddy Waters, though it's been covered by many people. This line is not the same as the original version, but it's how it typically gets played. The variation shown matches up with a few recorded versions of the tune, so double check with someone about which lick is used for the stops.

Hoochie Coochie Man

TRACK 39

Stops Variation

This song is one of the all-time great blues hits. Even though B.B. King already had a long and illustrious career, this tune made him a household name in the late 1960s. "The Thrill Is Gone" is called on at gigs all the time, and because it has unique changes and a specific feel, it's important to learn. Bassist Jerry Jemmott played on the original track and put every ounce of soul he had into it. His persistent, throbbing rhythmic figure had a lot to do with this song's success. The tune is built on a minor blues progression, which substitutes minor 7th chords for the I and IV. Instead of going straight to the V chord in measure 9, there is a ♭VImaj7 chord (in this key it's a Gmaj7) dropping to a Vsus4 (F♯sus4) which then resolves to the V (F♯7).

The Thrill Is Gone

TRACK 40

Another great minor blues is "All Your Love (I Miss Loving)" by Otis Rush. It's an F# minor blues (though the key may vary) played with a rhumba feel. Notice that it stays on the V chord for measures 9 and 10 using a typical Latin-style line starting on G#. The stop in measure 12 is for the vocals. When solos are played through the form, continue the groove with the basic pattern. The original recording goes to a jump blues feel after a few choruses, playing a standard boogie line in F#.

All Your Love (I Miss Loving)

TRACK 41

"Farther up the Road" was made popular by Bobby "Blue" Bland. It has a signature lick for the intro, and then goes to a swinging shuffle line for the melody and solos. There are stops in measures 10 and 12 during the melody. For solos, play straight through. After the melody comes back, there is a little "rave up" at the end of the chorus in measures 11 and 12, and the out chorus is the intro figure extended into a blues form.

Farther up the Road

TRACK 42

Out Chorus

"Sweet Home Chicago" is played at every blues jam or gig. It's the national anthem of blues. It's a straight-ahead boogie shuffle in E. The opening chorus has a quick IV, followed by two choruses of stops. After the stops, the solos are on a standard long I form. After the solos, go back to the stops, then back to the first chorus (quick IV) to take it home.

We've used some new chart directions to indicate this form. First, you should make a mental note of the S-shaped sign and the *To Coda* mark, but play right past them the first time. When you finally see *D.S.* (dal segno, meaning "from the sign") *al Coda*, you jump back to the sign, play until the *To Coda* mark, and then jump down to the actual *Coda* ("tail"). That's a lot of jumping around, making it easy to get lost, so be sure to look for these symbols first if someone hands you a chart on a gig.

Sweet Home Chicago

TRACK 43

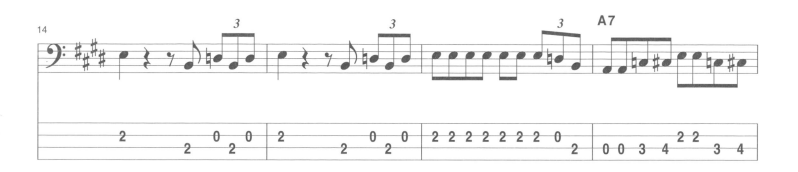

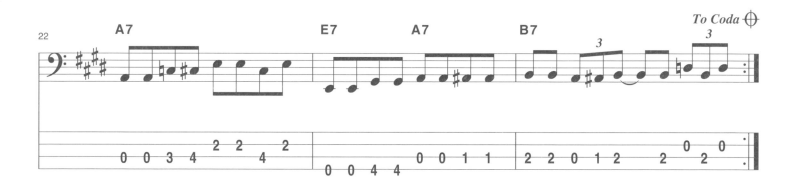

Guitar Solo

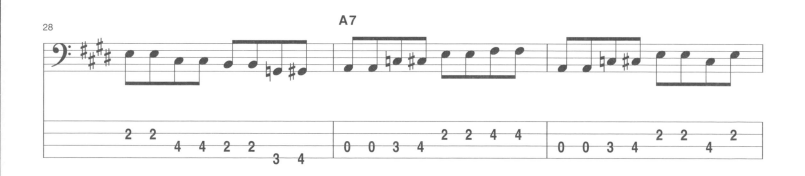

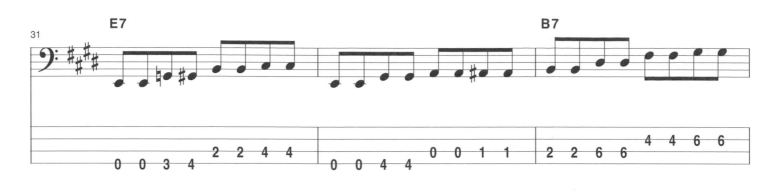

D.S. al Coda

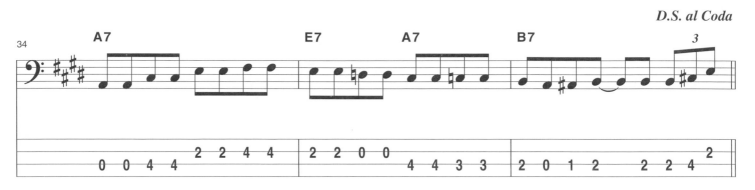

⊕ *Coda*

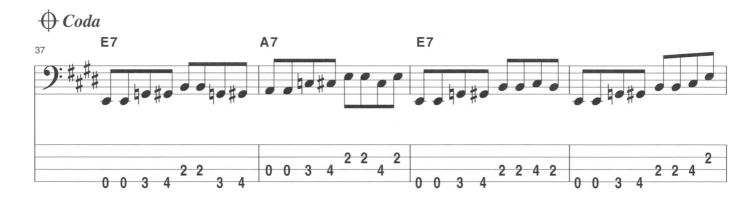

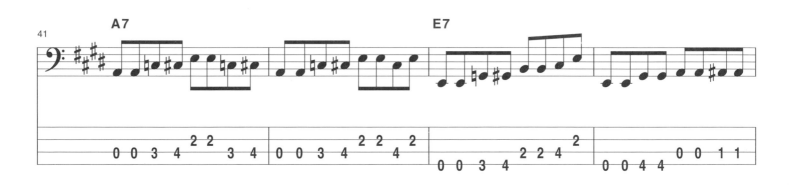

Straight Eighths

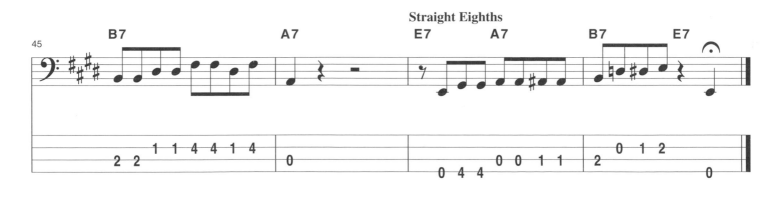

THOUGHTS ON BLUES BASS PLAYING

It's important to remember the role of the bass in blues. You are the foundation, the pulse, and the glue that holds it together. The lines and information in this book are what you need to know to do the job the way people expect it to be done, but it's still up to you to approach this style with an effective attitude. The blues is not about the bass player being the center of attention (unless you're singing too). The singer and soloists are the main focus, and it's best for you to leave the glory to them. Where we derive our greatest thrill in blues is the feeling we create when we lock in with the drums and make everyone play better than they ever imagined they could. It's the feeling of the energy coming back to you from the other band members and the audience. It's the satisfaction you get from knowing you played the style authentically and with feeling. Notice the word "feeling" comes up a lot. Well, the blues ain't nothin' but a feelin'—that's right!

ABOUT THE AUTHOR

Ed Friedland has written many well-received instructional books for bass, including the Hal Leonard *Electric Bass Method, Second Edition*. He wrote for *Bass Player Magazine* from 1992 to 2005. He is currently Senior Editor of *Guitar World's Bass Guitar Magazine*. He has taught at Berklee College of Music, Arizona State University, and Boston College, as well as privately since 1980. He has played with many great artists in jazz, rock, blues, theater, classical, Latin, country, and just about every style. His blues credentials include performances with Robert Junior Lockwood, Mighty Sam McClain, Robben Ford, Linda Hopkins, Johnny Adams, Paul Rishell, Annie Raines, Bruce Katz, Jim Kelly, David Maxwell, and Mike Williams, among others, as well as leading his own group, Lazy Ed & The Stratoloungers. Check out *www.edfriedland.com* for many free lessons, samples of Ed's books and basses, and much more.

HAL LEONARD BASS METHOD

HAL LEONARD BASS METHOD BOOK 1
SECOND EDITION
BY ED FRIEDLAND

METHOD BOOKS

by Ed Friedland

BOOK 1
Book 1 teaches: tuning; playing position; musical symbols; notes within the first five frets; common bass lines, patterns and rhythms; rhythms through eighth notes; playing tips and techniques; more than 100 great songs, riffs and examples; and more! The audio includes 44 full-band tracks for demonstration or play-along.
00695067 Book Only $7.99
00695068 Book/Online Audio.............................. $12.99

BOOK 2
Book 2 continues where Book 1 left off and teaches: the box shape; moveable boxes; notes in fifth position; major and minor scales; the classic blues line; the shuffle rhythm; tablature; and more!
00695069 Book Only $7.99
00695070 Book/Online Audio.............................. $12.99

BOOK 3
With the third book, progressing students will learn more great songs, riffs and examples; sixteenth notes; playing off chord symbols; slap and pop techniques; hammer-ons and pull-offs; playing different styles and grooves; and more.
00695071 Book Only $7.99
00695072 Book/Online Audio.............................. $12.99

COMPOSITE
This money-saving edition contains Books 1, 2 and 3.
00695073 Book Only $17.99
00695074 Book/Online Audio.............................. $24.99

DVD
Play your favorite songs in no time with this DVD! Covers: tuning, notes in first through third position, rhythms through eighth notes, fingerstyle and pick playing, 4/4 and 3/4 time, and more! Includes 6 full songs and on-screen music notation. 68 minutes.
00695849 DVD $19.95

BASS FOR KIDS
by Chad Johnson

Bass for Kids is a fun, easy course that teaches children to play bass guitar faster than ever before. Popular songs such as "Crazy Train," "Every Breath You Take," "A Hard Day's Night" and "Wild Thing" keep kids motivated, and the clean, simple page layouts ensure their attention remains focused on one concept at a time.
00696449 Book/Online Audio $12.99

REFERENCE BOOKS

BASS SCALE FINDER
by Chad Johnson

Learn to use the entire fretboard with the *Bass Scale Finder*. This book contains over 1,300 scale diagrams for the most important 17 scale types.
00695781 6" x 9" Edition...................................... $7.99
00695778 9" x 12" Edition.................................... $7.99

BASS ARPEGGIO FINDER
by Chad Johnson

This extensive reference guide lays out over 1,300 arpeggio shapes. 28 different qualities are covered for each key, and each quality is presented in four different shapes.
00695817 6" x 9" Edition..................................... $7.99
00695816 9" x 12" Edition.................................... $7.99

MUSIC THEORY FOR BASSISTS
by Sean Malone

Acclaimed bassist and composer Sean Malone will explain the written language of music, using easy-to-understand terms and concepts, diagrams, and much more. The audio provides 96 tracks of examples, demonstrations, and play-alongs.
00695756 Book/Online Audio $17.99

STYLE BOOKS

BASS LICKS
by Ed Friedland

This comprehensive supplement to any bass method will help students learn over 200 great bass licks, lines and grooves in many rhythmic styles. *Bass Licks* illustrates how simple melodic patterns can become the springboard for group improvisation or the foundation of a song.
00696035 Book/Online Audio $14.99

BASS LINES
by Matt Scharfglass

500 expertly written bass lines, riffs and fills in a wide variety of musical genres are included in this comprehensive collection to help players expand their bass vocabulary. The examples cover many tempos, keys and feels, and include easy bass lines for beginners on up to advanced riffs for more experienced bassists.
00148194 Book/Online Audio $19.99

BLUES BASS
by Ed Friedland

Learn to play studying the songs of B.B. King, Stevie Ray Vaughan, Muddy Waters, Albert King, the Allman Brothers, T-Bone Walker, and many more. Learn riffs from blues classics including: Born Under a Bad Sign • Hideaway • Hoochie Coochie Man • Killing Floor • Pride and Joy • Sweet Home Chicago • The Thrill Is Gone • and more.
00695870 Book/Online Audio $14.99

COUNTRY BASS
by Glenn Letsch

21 songs, including: Act Naturally • Boot Scootin' Boogie • Crazy • Honky Tonk Man • Love You Out Loud • Luckenbach, Texas (Back to the Basics of Love) • No One Else on Earth • Ring of Fire • Southern Nights • Streets of Bakersfield • Whose Bed Have Your Boots Been Under? • and more.
00695928 Book/Online Audio $17.99

FRETLESS BASS
by Chris Kringel

18 songs, including: Bad Love • Continuum • Even Flow • Everytime You Go Away • Hocus Pocus • I Could Die for You • Jelly Roll • King of Pain • Kiss of Life • Lady in Red • Tears in Heaven • Very Early • What I Am • White Room • more.
00695850.. $19.99

FUNK BASS
by Chris Kringel

This is your complete guide to learning the basics of grooving and soloing funk bass. Songs include: Can't Stop • I'll Take You There • Let's Groove • Stay • What Is Hip • and more.
00695792 Book/Online Audio.............................. $22.99

R&B BASS
by Glenn Letsch

This book/audio pack uses actual classic R&B, Motown, soul and funk songs to teach you how to groove in the style of James Jamerson, Bootsy Collins, Bob Babbitt, and many others. The 19 songs include: For Once in My Life • Knock on Wood • Mustang Sally • Respect • Soul Man • Stand by Me • and more.
00695823 Book/Online Audio $17.99

ROCK BASS
by Sean Malone

This book/audio pack uses songs from a myriad of rock genres to teach the key elements of rock bass. Includes: Another One Bites the Dust • Beast of Burden • Money • Roxanne • Smells like Teen Spirit • and more.
00695801 Book/Online Audio.............................. $21.99

SUPPLEMENTARY SONGBOOKS

These great songbooks correlate with Books 1-3 of the *Hal Leonard Bass Method*, giving students great songs to play while they're still learning! The audio tracks include great accompaniment and demo tracks.

EASY POP BASS LINES
20 great songs that students in Book 1 can master. Includes: Come as You Are • Crossfire • Great Balls of Fire • Imagine • Surfin' U.S.A. • Takin' Care of Business • Wild Thing • and more.
00695810 Book Only $9.99
00695809 Book/Online Audio.............................. $15.99

MORE EASY POP BASS LINES
20 great songs for Level 2 students. Includes: Bad, Bad Leroy Brown • Crazy Train • I Heard It Through the Grapevine • My Generation • Pride and Joy • Ramblin' Man • Summer of '69 • and more.
00695819 Book Only $12.99
00695818 Book/Online Audio.............................. $16.99

EVEN MORE EASY POP BASS LINES
20 great songs for Level 3 students, including: ABC • Another One Bites the Dust • Brick House • Come Together • Higher Ground • Iron Man • The Joker • Sweet Emotion • Under Pressure • more.
00695821 Book $9.99
00695820 Book/Online Audio.............................. $16.99

HAL•LEONARD

Visit Hal Leonard online at
www.halleonard.com